Montgomery & the River Region Sketchbook

Indigo Custom Publishing

Publisher	Henry S. Beers
Project Coordinator	Bill Koons
Editor-in-Chief	Martha Elrod
Art Director/Designer	Jennifer Shermer Pack
Graphic Designer	Daniel Emerson
Operations Manager	Gary Pulliam
Associate Publisher	Richard J. Hutto

© 2004 by Indigo Custom Publishing

All rights reserved. No part of this book may be reproduced in any form or by any means without prior written permission from the publisher, except for brief quotations used in reviews written specifically for inclusion in a magazine, newspaper, or broadcast media.

Printed in Hong Kong

Library of Congress Control Number: 2004116299

ISBN: 097628751X

Indigo custom books are available at quantity discounts
with bulk purchase for educational, business, or sales promotional use.
For information, please write to:
Indigo Custom Publishing, 3920 Ridge Avenue, Macon, GA 31210, or call 866-311-9578.

Montgomery & the River Region Sketchbook

Paintings by Local Artists • Author, Mary Ann Neeley

6 Introduction

8 River Region Heritage

33 Montgomery and Montgomery County

57 Autauga, Elmore, Lowndes and Macon Counties

79 Life in the River Region

Adams Hudson

The Artists

Front row: Carol Barksdale Meredith, Karen Seamon, Melissa B. Tubbs, Jane L. Jacobs, Karin E. Johns, Catherine Cope, Paulette Riley
Middle row: Bonnie Phillips, Richard Millman, Adams Hudson, Joseph Stone, Mary Campbell McLemore, Donnave Lindsey, Wendy A. Slaton, Cam Walker, Ann C. Carmichael, Betty Pinkston
Back row: Neal Brantley, John W. Feagin, Connie Watts, Shirley Esco, Bob Adams, David Keith Braly, Kathy McLeod, Tim Vaught, Mary Walton Upchurch

Introduction

Children of the War of 1812 and the Industrial Revolution, Montgomery and the other counties of the River Region stand on lands once the domain of the Creek Confederacy, a loosely organized grouping composed of several different Native American tribes based along the Coosa, Tallapoosa and Alabama rivers. Spain, France and England had competed for the territory from the sixteenth century until after the American Revolution.

This Alabama Frontier was a crossroads where cultures met and exchanged goods and ideas. When the Europeans arrived, they brought with them metal products, textiles, guns, ammunition and 'demon' rum. The Creeks had deerskins and hickory nut oils, both desirable trade goods, but more importantly, they occupied lands that the foreign powers desperately wanted and each in turn claimed as their own. The goods proffered by the intruders inevitably changed the life-style of the natives, tantalizing and seducing many with promises of more to come in return for trade and land cessions. The French built Fort Toulouse at the confluence of the Coosa and Tallapoosa rivers about 1717, but English and Scot traders were in the neighborhood soon thereafter. At the end of the French-Indian War in 1763, the English reigned supreme, but the revolt of their colonists divided loyalties within the tribes. When the Revolutionary War ended, the Creeks, who, for the most part had remained loyal to the English, found themselves in a precarious position as their old friends packed up and sailed for home. A young leader, however, emerged; half Scot and half Indian, Alexander McGillivray assumed a position that enabled him to seek help from the Spanish who now occupied West Florida. Promising to protect Spanish interests from the encroaching Americans, McGillivray, in return, received trade goods from the Spanish. When Spain failed to come through on its part of the bargain, the Creek leader had them admit an English trading firm into Pensacola to supply the Indians' needs.

The next few years brought continuing controversy between the Creeks and the land-hungry, restless Americans on what was then the southwest frontier. In 1790, George Washington issued an invitation to McGillivray and other Creek leaders to come to New York, then capital of the new country, for a conference. For McGillivray, this was something of a triumph as he and his fellow Creeks received a warm welcome while refusing to give too much ground to their

Drawn by A. R. Waud
Courtesy of Stonehenge Gallery

Distance view of riverboat on the Alabama River approaching the city in mid-1800s.

hosts. The wily McGillivray returned home with a brigadiership in the United States Army, an annual stipend and a secret trade agreement. Three years later, however, McGillivray was dead, and a new chapter in Creek-American relations had begun. The next twenty years saw a steady deterioration in the relationship that culminated with the Creeks and the Americans fighting a frontier war within the War of 1812.

The Americans ambitiously and continuously pressed onto the frontier, yearning for the Creeks' land that was almost perfect for the growing of the short staple cotton, a fiber in great demand because of the mechanization of the textile industry and the development of the cotton gin. Although a long staple cotton grew along the coastal regions of Georgia and South Carolina, it could not begin to satisfy the demand for cotton. But the interior lands of these states, into Alabama and on westward, were ideal for the short staple type.

In 1805, following the acquisition of Louisiana, the United States negotiated a treaty with the Creeks for a road through their territory that would be a link in a postal connection between New Orleans and Washington. Of course, others, in addition to the post riders, used the road that provided access for intruders and settlers in the region. As tensions heightened between the natives and these people, the Shawnee leader Tecumseh arrived, calling for war against the white man. Those who adhered to his cause, the Red Sticks, attacked Fort Mims, a settlers' fortification, killing a large number and launching a series of encounters that brought the wrath of the American militia down upon them.

The 1814 Battle of Horseshoe Bend forced the proud Native Americans to their knees as Andrew Jackson, the victor, demanded and received a land cession of some 30,000,000 acres in Alabama and western Georgia. The Alabama Creeks reserved land east of the Coosa and west of the Chattahoochee rivers for their homeland.

The River Region

The counties that today compose the River Region of Central Alabama, with the exception of

Courtesy of Stonehenge Gallery

Macon County, were all a part of this original cession. Montgomery County, organized in 1816, bears the name of Major Lemuel P. Montgomery and was much larger originally, but donated much of its land for the creation of neighboring counties. One of the earliest of these was Autauga County that came into existence in 1818 bearing the name of a creek and the Indian village of Atagi. Lowndes County, named for William Lowndes, a South

February 18, 1861. Jefferson Davis was sworn in as president of the Confederate States of America on the State Capitol portico. On March 4 the first national flag of the Confederacy was raised over the capitol.

Carolina statesman, and created from parts of Montgomery, Dallas and Butler County, dates from 1830. The Alabama Legislature created Macon County, honoring Revolutionary hero Nathaniel Macon, in 1832 from a part of the last Creek land cession. Elmore County, named for early settler John Archer Elmore, has existed since 1866 when the Legislature apportioned parts of Coosa, Autauga, Tallapoosa and Montgomery counties for its creation.

Alabama Fever

When the newly acquired lands went on sale at Milledgeville, Georgia, in 1817, people from the eastern states rushed to put down payments on choice parcels of the fertile territory. Alabama Fever raged with such symptoms as the overwhelming urge to buy land, plant cotton, and get rich. Promoters had noted the Big Bend in the Alabama River as some of the finest lands in the entire cession, and many were eager to purchase portions of it. In what is now Montgomery County, several communities sprang up as people grasped the opportunities offered by the availability of land and promises of bountiful cotton crops. On the eastern boundary, Line Creek separated the county from the Creek Nation. The rolling land west of the creek attracted settlers even before the land sales at Milledgeville officially opened up the region. Pioneers, some veterans of the Creek American War, having seen the country and realizing its potential, gathered up families and whatever goods they could muster and returned to Montgomery County with visions of cotton dancing in their heads. Others, hearing of this Eden, rushed to be among the first. Georgians and Carolinians arriving over the Federal Road, and founded two prosperous villages, Line Creek (Waugh) and Mount Meigs. At the latter, the road veered to the southwest and near its junction with

Richard Millman

Oak Park was the first public park in Montgomery. This Pavillion, dating back to the early 1900s, was a popular center for social events like "Script Dances"—where a sheet would be posted in downtown businesses advertising a dance, and boys would sign up on the "script" (with the girl's name they would bring).

Pintlala Creek another village, named Pintlala, developed. As the County's population grew, other villages and communities came into being.

Andrew Dexter, a visionary but unsuccessful Massachusetts lawyer, bought a fractional section and to the northwest of him a consortium of Georgia land developers, led by General John Scott, put their money on a bluff of the Alabama River. Soon two villages were eyeing each other and competing for settlers. Andrew Dexter's New Philadelphia attracted merchants as well as settlers while the Georgian's Alabama Town had a jail, a school, and settlers but no merchants. To solve their plight, the latter bought land adjacent to New Philadelphia and established East Alabama Town.

Birth of a Town

Competition continued, but by 1819 both towns realized that they had better chances of succeeding if they united. With that in mind, they petitioned the Alabama Legislature meeting in Huntsville to incorporate them as the Town of Montgomery. On December 3, 1819, bearing the name of Revolutionary War General Richard Montgomery, the new village came into being. The Town of Montgomery had a population of four hundred and one when eligible voters turned out in January for the election of a city council that in turn chose an intendant from amongst themselves. They selected William Graham, a native of North Carolina and a New Philadelphia merchant, for the office. The municipal authorities immediately began formulating laws and establishing a tax base for the conducting of necessary business.

Montgomery flourished in its role of a trade and transportation center for the plantations, farms and communities springing up throughout the region.

Richard Millman

The steamboat Alabama *was one of many riverboats that docked at Montgomery in the 1800s to load both freight and passengers.*

Pole boats carried cotton down the Alabama River to Mobile for shipment to the mills in Europe and New England, then brought goods back up river for planters and merchants. In October, 1821, the arrival of the steamboat Harriett ushered in an exciting new method of moving goods and people in Central Alabama, enhancing Montgomery's economic position in the state.

Culturally, the town was also growing with a newspaper, The Montgomery Republican, that later changed its name to the Alabama Journal, enlightening the citizenry; also, churches, schools and a theatrical group contributed to the ideals of elevating the mind, spirit and body. By 1830, there was a theatre on Washington Street where traveling troupes frequently performed.

A few miles down the Alabama River, the county seat of Autauga County, Washington, flourished for a few years, but later the county moved its seat inland to Kingston. Another village, however, soon surpassed it. In the early 1830s New Englander Daniel Pratt, a builder of cotton gins, founded Prattville on the Autauga Creek where he harnessed its waters for the production of gins that became world renowned. Pratt, Alabama's first industrialist, also established a cotton mill, iron foundry, and millworks. Today, his buildings on the bank of Autauga Creek house Continental Eagle that continues to manufacture gins for the international market. Other entrepreneurs, intrigued by the idea of using steam to move vehicles on tracks, organized a company in the early 1830s to build a railroad to West Point, Georgia. Although it took nearly twenty years to reach its goal, it did carry goods and passengers to and from Montgomery as it inched its way across the eastern reaches of the state.

Richard Millman

The Old Montgomery Courthouse (1894), located at Washington and Lawerence streets, was the seat of county government until the 1950s.

11

Indian Removal

Since the Creek Indians had kept for themselves the area east of the Coosa River, there had been discussions about moving them west for resettlement. Treaties signed between the United States government and the Native Americans in the early 1830s encouraged the quick dispatching of them so that Americans could claim the land. By 1836-37, the Creeks and their fellow Indians were gone, and many of their former hunting grounds were under cultivation, much of it for the growing of cotton.

The young state's population was spreading out into the Black Belt, south and west of Montgomery, and into the lands to the east, formerly the home of the Creeks. The removal of the Native Americans opened the way for the creation of Macon County and the development of its seat, Tuskegee, a cotton marketing town that in the 1850s became a center for education with several schools including Tuskegee Female College and the East Alabama Female College. In the 1880s, Booker T. Washington founded Tuskegee Institute for the education of African-Americans; now Tuskegee University, the world-renowned school serves a broad spectrum of students.

In the 1830s, Hayneville won the seat of government of Lowndes County and today an outstanding ante-bellum courthouse continues to serve its citizens. A few miles away the planters' town of Lowndesboro, a mecca of pre-Civil War activities and education, still harbors over thirty buildings from that era.

Cotton and Slavery

Cotton had brought men to the region and for its cultivation many hands were necessary. Slavery answered this need with hundreds of African-Americans working the fields throughout

Richard Millman

Figh-Picket-Barnes School House, c. 1837, is the oldest surviving brick dwelling in Montgomery. Moved from its original site, it now stands at the corner of Mildred and South Court streets where it is the home of the Montgomery County Historical Society and the Montgomery Museum of History.

Central Alabama. The Black Belt region, just to the south and west of Montgomery, supported the biggest plantations and, hence, the largest number of African slaves. In North Alabama, the Tennessee River Delta also boasted large plantations and numerous slaves. Yet, only about 30 percent of Alabamians owned slaves but for some segments of the population the major goal was the owning of many acres of land and slaves to work it. Others struggled with what to do with the slaves they had inherited, and some even freed their bondsmen in bursts of generosity or guilt.

Capturing the Capital

Alabama had entered the state on December 14, 1819, with the first capital, Cahaba, at the junction of the Alabama and Cahaba rivers. This location, with which north Alabamians were unhappy, was susceptible to floods and their associated diseases. By 1826, this combination of political discontent, rising waters and sickness had persuaded the legislature to move the seat of government to Tuscaloosa, in the western quadrant of the state. Montgomery, whose founder Andrew Dexter envisioned it as the capital, urged lawmakers to bring it here, where the hill at the eastern end of Market Street, given by Dexter to the town with stipulations that the state would receive it when Montgomery became capital, awaited its crown.

The rise, upon which town goats grazed, had to wait a few more years for its coronation.

With the exodus of the Native Americans and the influx of settlers to the newly formed eastern counties, the geographic and demographic centers of Alabama shifted dramatically; the Tuscaloosa capital was

Joseph Stone

At the current site of Maxwell Air Force Base the Wright Brothers established the nation's first civilian flying school in 1910. They also made the first recorded night flight.

now far to the west, causing unhappiness because of its distance from many areas and the difficulty in getting to it. An 1845 referendum won voters' permission to again move the capital, and in the legislative session of January, 1846, heated debate and sixteen rounds of votes finally rewarded Montgomery with the prize; it had at last captured the capital.

A story often told about the contest for the capital related that the menu for the dining room of the Exchange Hotel had been the deciding factor in determining the site as resourceful Montgomery lobbyists circulated a paper through the legislative chambers listing the gourmet offerings of the hostelry. Perhaps the way to a legislator's vote was through his stomach. Another more immediate enticement for the state was that of Montgomery businessmen offering to float a $75,000 bond issue that would provide funds to build the capitol at no cost to the state on the rise known as "Goat Hill."

Another strong contender for the capital was Wetumpka; founded in 1834, it straddled the Coosa River northeast of Montgomery. The town had many of the same advantages as Montgomery, including ready access by river and a thriving, growing population with political and business leaders eager to acquire the capital. The state had located its first penitentiary there in 1839, and many thought it should also be the site of Alabama's government.

When word finally arrived in Montgomery on January 30, 1846, wild and jubilant celebrations broke out, climaxed by the firing of one hundred cannon rounds by the True Blue Militia from Goat Hill. Immediately plans got underway to issue and sell the bonds and to choose an architect for the state house. A competition resulted in the selection of Stephen Decatur Button as the designer; although a northerner, Button was working in Columbus, Georgia, at the time. By June, 1847, construction was underway and on July 4, the Masonic Orders laid the cornerstone with great fanfare and ceremony. In December, the handsome Greek Revival building welcomed the legislature to its new chambers with general approbation and acclaim from them and the public as a whole. Unfortunately, two years later, December 14, 1849, the beautiful "Temple of Democracy" burned to the ground.

Progress and Prosperity

The decade of the 1850s opened on a sad note as the legislature faced the problem of re-building the state house or, as some suggested, moving the capital back to Tuscaloosa or some other town. Montgomery won, retaining the seat of government, but the city did not offer to again pay for the capitol. The state allocated $60,000 for its reconstruction on the foundations of the original structure. In 1851, a handsome building once again graced "Goat Hill;" however, this one did not have quite as many decorative touches as had the first.

There was another major accomplishment in 1851 when the Montgomery and West Point Railroad finally crossed the Chattahoochee River, connecting Montgomery with railroads to other parts of the nation. New goods and people arrived in Montgomery, bringing with them fresh ideas, vibrant energies and investment capital. Steamboat whistles reverberated off the river, trains rattled and hissed and wagons and carriages creaked and groaned as they bounced over the new plank roads; all these noises were music to the ears of a town eager to move forward as it recognized a need for self-improvement. An increasing awareness brought on a sophistication in architecture, public services, education, and entertainment.

Capitol architect Stephen Decatur Button may receive credit for introducing a sense of style as he designed at least two residences while in town in the late 1840s, both for members of the Capitol Building Commission. The magnificent Greek Revival Knox Hall on South Perry Street and the Pollard Mansion on Jefferson Street reflected the fashion of the times and the growing affluence of Montgomery's entrepreneurs. William Knox was a businessman, planter and banker while Charles Pollard was the driving force behind railroad development. Others followed their lead and soon the city's residential streets sported stylish Greek Revival and Italianate residences, large and small.

Ordeman Shaw House
Joseph Stone

The crown jewel of Old Alabama Town and its first restoration, the 1850s Ordeman Townhouse exemplifies the life of the upper-middle class of that time with its high style furnishings and the unusual feature of a partial basement with dining rooms.

Carol Barksdale Meredith

On William Bartram's grand excursion through the southeast in the mid-1770s, he sketched the Creek Indian Village of Tukabatchie on the Tallapoosa River in Elmore County.

Churches, formerly rather simple frame structures, also caught the building fever. First Presbyterian led the way with a Gothic style brick edifice in 1847 followed by the Methodist Church's classical revival brick building in 1852. St. Peter's Catholic Church elected the Romanesque style for its house of worship in 1854, and St. John's Episcopal Church, designed by the New York firm of Wills and Dudley, was in the Gothic motif. The commercial sector, feeling the need to stay abreast of the latest styles, indulged in such beauties as the Romanesque Revival Central Bank of Alabama across Market Street from the earlier Winter Building, the Montgomery Theatre and, of course, the Greek Revival Exchange Hotel on Court Square.

The city and county, not to be outdone, caught the enthusiasm. The county moved the Court House from its site at the western end of Market Street on the Square to the corner of Washington and Lawrence streets where it had architect Charles Ordeman design a classical revival new seat of county government. The city, spurred on by business interests, beautified Court Square by digging out the artesian well and creating a basin surrounded by a decorative iron fence.

Technology also contributed to the city's advancements with business interests providing the financing for a water works, gas lights and a telegraph service. An omnibus transported goods and people from boats and trains around town, but the plank road investments proved futile as the roadways were much more expensive to build and maintain than anticipated.

Other areas in the River Region also experienced a building boom in the 1840s and 1850s. Around Prattville and Wetumpka, a number of homes reflected the influence of

Daniel Pratt who had earlier worked as a builder in Savannah, Georgia. Two story houses with central, columned porticos graced plantations and town lanes; perhaps not as lavish as Pratt's own home, these houses did bear some of its characteristics. Tuskegee sported similar houses, both large and small, but its Gray Pillars and the Thompson Mansion were two of the finest examples of late Greek Revival and its incorporation with the new Italianate style. Certainly not to be outshone by its neighbors, Lowndes County, too, demonstrated the talents of its builders with courthouse, homes and churches. It was a period of prosperity, and the houses of planters, entrepreneurs, professionals and the average citizen illustrated general well-being and growing aspirations.

Cotton continued to drive the economy and when the crop was good, everyone prospered. Even during the national economic depression of 1857, the fiber enabled the South to ride out the panic with less loss of revenue than other sections of the country. With an over-confidence in the world-wide demand for cotton, southerners viewed the future with optimism.

Yet the question of slavery became more prominent as northern abolitionists gained strength and political influence; southern planters, too, had political voices, not always attuned to those of the other sections. Perhaps the most vocal of these was a Montgomery lawyer, William Lowndes Yancey, who led the Alabama delegation to the Democratic Convention of 1860 vowing to walk out if his demands were not met for governmental protection for the property of southerners who ventured into territories outside the slave-holding states. True to his word, fire-brand Yancey did march out, breaking up the convention when he did not get his way. The nomination of Abraham Lincoln for president by the free-soil Republican Party brought derision from southerners who determined to secede from the Union if he won the election.

Richard Millman

Original Executive Residence of President Jefferson Davis and his family, from February 1861 to May of the same year, when the Confederate Capital was moved to Richmond.

Secession, Confederacy and War

As is well-known, Abe did win the election of 1860, and southern states hastened to secede, with Alabama issuing an invitation to them to meet in Montgomery in January, 1861. Gathering in Alabama's capitol, the delegates organized the Confederate States of America, chose Jefferson Davis as its provisional president and Montgomery as its provisional capital. Confederate hopes of leaving the Union peacefully were not to be and on April 11, the Confederate cabinet sent a message from the telegraph office in the Winter Building ordering General Beauregard in Charleston Harbor to remove the federal troops from Fort Sumter. The bombardment of the United States' facility ushered in four years of conflict.

For the first three months, Montgomery hosted thousands of military, political, and legislative personnel and hopeful office seekers, but in May, the Confederate government moved to Richmond, Virginia, to be closer to what it presumed would be the main scenes of battle. Montgomery and other towns in the region vigorously assumed their new roles as suppliers of men and materials. In Montgomery railroad shops, a small rifle manufactory, nitre works and even a boat yard that launched at least one boat, the Nashville, supported the war effort.

In January, 1865 Union general James H. Wilson led his cavalry corps from North Alabama on a campaign to destroy all facilities capable of producing war materials with his ultimate goal the destruction of the Selma Arsenal, second only to the Tredegar Iron Works in Richmond. Wilson and his men moved swiftly with one unit advancing on Tuscaloosa where they burned the University of Alabama and others fanning out to such iron producing foundries as Briarfield and Tannehill. Arriving at Selma, Wilson's forces met fierce but futile opposition; Selma fell and the next destination was Montgomery.

Carol Barksdale Meredith

In 1802 Abram Mordecai, a Jewish veteran of the Revolutionary War who settled in this area, installed Alabama's first cotton gin. The restored Thomas W. Oliver Gin in Old Alabama Town was originally manufactured by the Continental Gin Company in Prattville.

During the war the Union blockade and the Confederate embargo had prevented the shipping of cotton, so Central Alabama planters and farmers sent their crops to Montgomery warehouses for storage until that grand day when the markets were again available. By April, 1865 there were possibly as many as 100,000 bales packed in local warehouses. With Union troops on the way, the small Confederate force in the Capital City eyed the cotton and with the consent of the city authorities ordered it torched so that it would not fall into enemy hands. On the afternoon of April 11 as the military unit departed, a warehouseman started the fires. As they raged, the mayor, council and several prominent citizens rode out to meet the approaching Union soldiers and surrender the town. The black volunteer firemen received great credit for their success in preventing the fires from spreading and burning the town. About 4 a.m. the next morning, Wilson's advance guard rode into town and up Market Street to the capitol where they removed the Confederate flag and replaced it with the flag of the United States. The burning of the railroad shops and other small industries by the Federals were acts of war, but the civilian population and the built environment suffered little as Wilson's men respected the terms of the surrender.

Joseph Stone

The War was over for Montgomery and its surrounding neighbors.

Reconstruction

The River Region, as well as the entire South, had to adjust to dramatic changes in the social, political and economic systems. For some it was a time of sadness for the loss of loved ones and the old way of life, but for others it was a time of rejoicing; freedom was at hand. Former slaves

In 1887, Montgomery became the first city in the Western Hemisphere to convert its entire street railway system to electricity. Having begun its initial operation in 1886, the historic "Lightning Route" trolleys continued unitl buses replaced them in 1936.

John Feagin

As pastor of the Dexter Avenue Baptist Church from 1954-60, Dr. Martin Luther King, Jr. became leader of the Montgomery Improvement Association that conducted the Montgomery Bus Boycott from December 1955 to November 1956. The congregation changed the name to the Dexter Avenue Memorial Baptist Church, memorializing their former minister after his 1968 death.

moved into towns from the surrounding countryside creating housing and labor problems. In 1860, Montgomery had a population of over 8,000, nearly half of whom were black and lived in masters' yards or in certain specified areas of town. Now, the influx of new-comers was causing wide-spread concern with people putting together makeshift housing out of any available material. In the northern part of town, the remains of the burned railroad shops provided materials for shelter including tin, wooden packing cases and abandoned railroad cars. The cold fall and winter of 1865 and the outbreak of smallpox among many new arrivals increased the hardships.

The cry of "Hard Times" echoed throughout the community, but there were signs, too, that the situation would improve. Help for the black population came from city authorities, the military, the Freedman's Bureau, the American Missionary Association, a wing of the Congregational Church, and ordinary citizens. African-American congregations organized and built churches such as the Baptist Church on Columbus Street (1867) St. John's AME on Madison Avenue (1871) and the Congregational Church at the corner of Union and High streets (1872). Old Ship AME Zion on Mildred Street had been an active congregation even before the Civil War, meeting in the 1830s building donated by the white Methodists when they were building a new church in 1852. These and other religious and secular groups provided leadership and assistance to a people bravely struggling to make their way in a new environment.

On the political scene, there was a definite change with a white Republican mayor and a council composed of blacks and whites. Among the former was Holland Thompson, who as chairman of the school board committee even-handedly supported the needs of black and white schools. By the mid-seventies, however, the tide was beginning to turn as old-line white political figures regained control. In Montgomery this effort included the gerrymandering of wards four and five with their majority black populations out of the city's electoral districts. Economically, the city was beginning to regain stability when the Panic of 1873 caused another period of financial distress but ever so gradually hard times began to give way to better days.

In the rural sectors life was often difficult as farmers struggled to adjust to new problems and labor situations. People who had land needed workers, and those without it, needed places to live and work, and from this situation emerged sharecropping. Blacks and whites turned to this method of livelihood, with cotton dominating as the cash crop, often to the detriment of the entire economic system. The National Grange for the Patrons of Husbandry, organized by the United States Department of Agriculture in the late 1860s, attempted to educate both farmers and families with its southern mission emphasizing crop diversification, the growing of more food stuffs and less cotton, and a wage for labor system. Although unsuccessful in weaning farmers away from cotton and disrupting the sharecropping system, it did provide co-operative means of buying farming goods and supplies. Another important effort involved working to get fair railroad rates for Alabama farmers

By the 1880s, people had settled into new modes of life and work. In the River Region, a new day was dawning, bringing prosperity to some and new hope to everyone.

Richard Millman

The Teague house, built early 1850s, was placed on the National Register of Historic Places in 1972 and later became the offices of the Alabama Historical Commission.

21

The 1880s

In many ways, the decade of the '80s resembled that of the 1850s, both periods of urbanization, civic pride and progress, with technology once again playing a significant role in the process. In 1881, the telephone announced its arrival with a constant jangling that continues to this day. In 1883, the city installation of tall Brush Arc electric lights around Court Square both amazed and frightened a population stunned by the use of electrical power. This was, of course, only the beginning of such an awesome source of energy for by 1885, the incandescent bulb was here and the practical illumination of residences and businesses became possible. Transportation, too, made strides because of the harnessing of electricity as a motive power.

In 1885, the Capital City Street Railway Company initiated streetcar service with "Jingle Bells," so called because of the bells worn around the necks of the small Texas mules that pulled the little cars. James A. Gaboury, manager of the company, however, had bigger plans and convinced a somewhat reluctant City Council to grant him a franchise for an electrically powered streetcar. "The Lightning Route" was in service by the spring of April, 1886 and the following year established Montgomery's place in transportation history with the company electrifying its entire fifteen mile route.

A building boom altered the streetscape in all sectors as residential, commercial and governmental structures introduced new techniques, styles and details. The Montgomery Advertiser noted in 1886 that "widely differing styles of new and elegant homes show that architecture is bound by no rules in producing pleasing effects...." This was quite true in the business and governmental departments as well. The many structures rising included the east wing on the capitol, the Federal

Carol Barksdale Meredith

The Shotgun House in Old Alabama Town represents a type of housing many African-Americans lived in as they moved into urban areas following the Civil War. It acquired the name "shotgun" because of its long narrow shape and the belief that a gun shot would go through every room of the house.

Courthouse on Dexter Avenue and the first "skyscraper," the Moses Building, on Court Square.

While the steady "hum of saw and clang of hammers" indicated the prosperity enjoyed by the citizens, the City also worked to enhance the quality of life with a new water works, hex block sidewalks, granite curbs and streets paved with vitrified brick and granite blocks. After much complaint about the "hog wallow in the Square," the City beautified the Artesian Basin with the Court Square Fountain, copied after the middle section of one the J.L. Mott Iron Works had made for California millionaire James Flood.

A fitting climax to the decade of the 1880s was the visit of Grover Cleveland, the first sitting president to visit Montgomery and also the first Democrat in the White House since the Civil War. It was an opportunity for the whole region to celebrate, for once again the citizens felt as though they were, indeed, full-fledged members of the United States.

Turn-of the Twentieth Century

Several events of the 1890s defined times to come, financially, socially and politically. The Panic of 1893 brought to a close most of the exuberance of the 1880s. In 1896, the Plessy vs. Ferguson ruling by the Supreme Court of "separate but equal eventually took away many of the new freedoms enjoyed by African-Americans. Hard on the heels of it, came the Spanish-American War with its outcome propelling the United States into a power on the international scene. On the local level, passengers on trains into and out of Montgomery welcomed the magnificent new Union Station and Train Shed. Built by the Louisville and Nashville Railroad, the complex consolidated all passenger service; rail lines then constructed freight terminals for goods. Only one of these still stands, the Western Freight Depot on Coosa Street that now is a part of the baseball stadium.

Cotton still had a firm grip on the economy as the twentieth century dawned, undergirding Montgomerians in the same ways it always had, while the warehouses and markets in Montgomery were reporting higher earnings than ever before. Wholesalers, too, were continuing to supply Central Alabama from their handsome business houses located in the Commerce Street district, close to river and rail. New buildings downtown added height to the skyline with the Bell Building and the First National Bank, both twelve stories tall, and the Gay-Teague Hotel of ten stories projecting the city skyward. In 1910, citizens looked up as the Wright Brothers established the nation's first civilian flying school on the western outskirts of town.

Again, Montgomery earned a spot in transportation annals with the flyers soaring and turning and even making a night flight or two during the school's three months of operation.

World War I

World War I brought flight again to Montgomery. The same land on which the Wrights had flown was ideal for military use, and the government established ARDMONT (Air Repair Depot Montgomery) to support the small flying fields scattered over the Southeast, one of which was Taylor Field in the country east of town. Montgomery also hosted a large infantry training facility, Camp Sheridan, northeast of town. Citizens rallied to the cause; men joined the services and women served the war effort in many capacities. Children, too, did their part, planting Victory Gardens and collecting scrap metal. When the War ended, the government closed Sheridan and Taylor Field, but retained Ardmont, renaming it Maxwell Field in the early 1920s.

Jazz Age

During the war, a popular local girl, Zelda Sayre, and a dashing officer stationed at Camp Sheridan, F. Scott Fitzgerald, met at a Country Club dance. Falling in love, the two married in 1920 as

Catherine Cope

Fitzgerald's first novel, This Side of Paradise, made the best seller list. Living extravagantly in New York and Europe they came to epitomize the Jazz Age. In Montgomery as well as in other nearby areas, flappers kicked up their heels and bootleg gin flowed, but local activities did not gain the same notoriety as Zelda's and Scott's.

Several Montgomery women, more or less contemporaries of Zelda's, made their marks on the literary, theatrical and artistic scene during the era. Sarah Haardt, who married journalist H.L. Mencken, was a writer of some renown while Anne Goldthwaite made her name in the art world.

Old wholesale warehousing found in Montgomery between the railroad and the river.

The actress Tallulah Bankhead, although not a native of Montgomery, spent time here with her aunt, Marie Bankhead Owen, director of the Alabama Department of Archives and History.

In Wetumpka, Kelly Fitzpatrick was painting the local scene, immortalizing the life of country and city folk in a period that retained many characteristics of the South that would disappear after the Depression and World War II.

The Great Depression

Montgomery expanded during the 1920s, incorporating the village of Cloverdale on the south and Capital Heights on the east. As the decade waned, however, ominous economic signs became more apparent leading up to the Stock Market Crash in October, 1929. The Great Depression was hard on the city, but because of state government and Maxwell Field, a degree of stability carried the town through. The coming of World War II helped the entire country overcome many economic problems, and Montgomery and the River Region were no exceptions.

World War II

In the 1930s, Montgomery built a municipal airport northeast of town and in 1940 leased it to the federal government for $1.00. When longtime Mayor W.A. Gunter died in 1941, the city named the field in his memory. Thus, when war came, Montgomery had two bases, Maxwell and Gunter, that were ready for military purposes. During the War, almost 100,000 pilots, navigators and bombardiers trained on these facilities. At the end of the conflict the Army Air Corps became the U.S. Air Force and both Maxwell and Gunter remained active. Within a few years, Maxwell became the Air University for the training of officers.

The civilian population worked round the clock in support of the war effort. Women went to work on flight lines, in factories, joined military units

David Braly

Andrew Carnegie invested much of his fortune creating public libraries across the country, and Montgomery's is an excellent example of the Beaux Arts Classicism prevalent in the early 20th century. Though now housing county offices, it still lends a genteel grace and jewel-like presence to Montgomery's architectural heritage.

and counted out their ration coupons. Men from the River Region served in every branch of the service; many did not return home.

Civil Rights

After the War, there were many changes, but for African-Americans some things had not changed; discrimination still prevailed in many areas including public transportation. In Montgomery, a growing discontent focused on the buses with complaints about rude drivers, flawed seating arrangements and lack of African-American drivers, particularly in black neighborhoods. On December 1, 1955, a seamstress, Mrs. Rosa Parks, got on a bus on Court Square and sat in a seat that could be used by either race if there were enough seats for whites. She rode one block and as more whites climbed aboard, the driver told her to get up; when she refused to do so, police arrested Mrs. Parks and took her to the police station. Calling E.D. Nixon, head of the local NAACP, she asked for help; Nixon in turn called white lawyer Clifford Durr and his wife, Virginia. When word spread, Alabama State Professor Jo Anne Robinson mimeographed a call for a bus boycott on Parks' court day, December 5. Ministers and laymen organized the Montgomery Improvement Association, electing Martin Luther King, Jr. the young minister of the Dexter Avenue Baptist Church as president, thus launching him on a career as leader of the modern Civil Rights Movement.

The boycott on December 5 was almost a total success, and at a mass meeting the crowd supported the idea of continuing it until the city and bus company agreed to rectify some of the problems. With no success along those lines, Attorney Fred Gray filed a federal law suit that resulted in the U.S. Supreme Court's November,

Rev. Tony Scott

The Tuskegee Airmen, African-American fighter pilots of the U.S. Army Corps who fought with distinction during World War II, were trained at the Tuskegee Army Air Field, in Macon County. As bomber escorts they never lost a bomber to enemy fighters, destroyed 251 enemy aircraft and won more then 850 medals. Sixty-six Tuskegee Airmen were killed in action.

1956, ruling that segregated seating on public transportation was illegal. This decision and the boycott led the way to many other efforts for civil rights including the Freedom Riders and the Selma-Montgomery Voting Rights March. There is a historical irony in Montgomery's role as birthplace of both Civil War and civil rights.

Growth and Change

Urban Renewal and the Interstates altered Montgomery's built environment and streetscape drastically as Interstate I-85 and I-65 intersected, decimating old neighborhoods, black and white, and forcing resettlement of thousands of people. Downtown struggled to stem the movement of shopping facilities to malls and strips, while it also witnessed the demolishing of structures and the re-configuring of streets. These shocking transformations in the city's senses of time and place triggered the preservation movement. Led by Landmarks Foundation of Montgomery, restortion efforts spread throughout the downtown and older residential neighborhoods. The urban renewal effort of the 1960s, however, did not succeed in its goal to maintain the center city as a merchandising arena. However, the preservation efforts resulted in the development of Old Alabama Town, the designating of local historic sites and the creation of historic districts. In the early years of the Twenty-First Century a new surge of downtown redevelopment, based to some extent around restoration and the re-development of the river front, promises to bring a further revitalization to the heart of town.

On the Cultural Scene

Culturally, Montgomery is a very diverse city with interests influenced by any number of factors including racial backgrounds, age and educational levels. A wide-range of talents and emotions offer richness to both the traditional and contemporary cultural scene.

There have been a number of significant musicians who were either native-born or migrated to this place. Although born Nathaniel Cole in Montgomery, Nat "King" Cole moved with his family to Chicago when he was two years old. Hank, Williams was a native of Mt. Olive, Alabama, south of Montgomery, but grew up in Greenville and Montgomery. Influenced by the black street musician "Teetot," young Williams developed his own style and won the hearts of millions with his lyrics and melodies. Others made their names in various musical genres. These included "Big Mama" Thornton and Clarence Carter in the blues world, and Nell Rankin who became a star on

Rev. Tony Scott

This unidentified lady represents the many women who walked to work or to catch a ride during the Montgomery Bus Boycott.

the operatic stage.

In 1930, the Montgomery Museum of Fine Arts, organized by local patrons, found a home in the old Girls High School on Lawrence and High Streets. Later, it joined the Montgomery Public Library in a new building on the same site. In the 1980s, the Museum moved to the Cultural Park, sharing beautiful grounds with the world-class Alabama Shakespeare Theatre, a magnanimous gift from construction magnate Wynton Blount. Downtown, Old Alabama Town, developed by Landmarks Foundation in conjunction with the City of Montgomery, is the South's premier outdoor history museum with fifty structures representing the architecture, history and culture of Central Alabama's nineteenth and early twentieth centuries.

Other River Region communities are also engaged in restoration and revitalization of their historic structures and their downtown areas. Prattville has a concerned citizenry and city leaders who recognize the significance of its place as the first industrial town in the state. The Autauga Heritage Association has restored an 1840s house as a museum, and on the same block the privately funded Pratt Village is a handsome complex of restored cottages, an 1840s hotel, now offices, and gardens. Individuals have joined the movement with the restoration of private homes in both towns

Melissa Tubbs

The Civil Rights Memorial, commissioned by the Southern Poverty Law Center and designed by Maya Lin, is a circular fountain containing a timeline of important events in the Civil Rights Movement. The engraved passage on the black granite walls is from Dr. Martin Luther Kings, Jr.'s "I Have A Dream" speech, part of the inspiration for the memorial.

Wetumpka, too, takes pride in its historic homes, churches and commercial structures. Located nearby is the redeveloped Fort Toulouse-Jackson that interprets both an eighteenth century French fort and a nineteenth century American outpost. Archaeologists still examine and study this site along the Coosa River, discovering and interpreting evidences of Native American, French, English and pioneer life. Within a few miles of it, the beautiful Jasmine Hill Gardens, located on the rim of a canyon made by a meteorite's prehistoric crash, recreate vestiges of Greece with temple, pool, and statuary set amidst lush, fragrant varieties of trees, shrubs and flowers. An 1830s preserved house is a focal point of this privately-owned cherished place that is frequently and generously shared with an appreciative public.

Lowndesboro and Hayneville have preserved important homes, churches and public buildings. Private residences dating from the 1830s line Lowndesboro's shady streets and main thoroughfare. Historic churches include those of the Episcopal, Presbyterian, Methodist and Baptist denominations. An inactive African-American church, recently restored by the Lowndesboro Historical Society, sports the copper cupola that once topped Alabama's first capital building in Cahaba.

In Macon County there are handsome private homes and commercial buildings, while structures on the campus of Tuskegee University comprise a National Park site. The 1850s Gray Pillars is home to the president of Tuskegee University and the Oaks, built by Tuskegee Institute students for its first president, Booker T. Washington, is open as a house museum. A number of buildings on the campus were also the work of students working under the direction of architects from the Institute. One of the most famous individuals associated with the school was George Washington Carver, botanist, agriculturist and inventor. An interesting campus museum interprets his work in the development of multiple uses for such common crops as the sweet potato and peanut. To him goes the credit for such a useful and tasty item as peanut butter, which he popularized as he promoted the cultivation of peanuts as an answer to the South's dependence on cotton. Downtown, a late nineteenth century courthouse stands guard over a typical square around which are early commercial houses.

This sampling of history and culture is just that—a taste of the rich heritage that underscores this region. Throughout it there are old cemeteries, churches, streams, fields and forests that contribute

Yvonne Williams

Home of Dr. Martin Luther King, Jr. and his family while pastoring Dexter Avenue Baptist Church during the Civil Rigths era. An incendiary device was thrown at the front of the house while Dr. King was at church; his family was fortunately in the rear of the house. Dr. King shortly thereafter calmed the crowd surrounding the house, and averted the probability of serious bloodshed.

to the senses of time and place that are so important to us, individually and collectively. We have immortalized our Native American heritage by adopting their names for rivers, creeks and locales, and in fields even today arrow heads, points and trade beads sometimes work their way to the top. In many still flow the proud blood of ancestral Creeks and other tribes. The French, too, have left an imprint on many, the memory of LaFayette and his visit in 1825 is still memorialized at Old Alabama Town's Lucas Tavern where he spent the night on the way into Montgomery. English, Scottish and Irish names are plentiful, reminding us that the British isles were points of departure for settlement in the New World. Our African-American heritage is present in the foods we eat and their preparation, and the expressions of speech which they introduced, enriching what we call "our mother tongue." Much of the built environment that we struggle to preserve was the work of slaves or, sometimes, free men of color. Today, we are indebted to the many cultures that merged in this Central Alabama River Region, and the many opportunities available for us to explore, expound upon and enjoy in this land so many of us call home.

Ruth Soffer

Rosa Parks at the groundbreaking ceremony for the Troy State of Montgomery Rosa Parks Library and Museum. Her refusal to relinquish her bus seat in the "white section," as well as her arrest and conviction, precipitated the beginning of the modern Civil Rights Movement.

Paulette Riley
Painting: Dexter Avenue, Court Square to the Capitol

Montgomery and Montgomery County

Bob Adams

Alabama Supreme Court

This was the scene of many notable legal decisions, most recently (2004) the removal of the Ten Commandments Monument placed there by a former Alabama Supreme Court Justice.

Sheridan Glenn

Alabama State Capitol

Alabama's capitol stands on Goat Hill, a site donated by town founder, Andrew Dexter, for the statehouse when Montgomery should become capital, a goal it achieved in 1846. The present 1856 Greek Revival building replaced an earlier one that burned in 1849. One of a very few state capitols designated as a National Historic Landmark, it has a magnificent dome decorated on the interior with murals depicting events in Alabama history.

Approaching Montgomery

Approaching Montgomery was an exciting part of the journey when the railways were in their prime. The train shed, built in 1897, was a noble structure then as now. Union Station with its bustling crowds of travelers was built the next year.

Paulette Riley

Mary Walton Upchurch

Early Morning on the Alabama River

Prior to the advent of rail transportation, the Alabama River — parallel to the railroad — was the main means of moving goods to and from Montgomery.

Karin Johns

Union Station

Union Station was the transportation center for Montgomery for many years, and now houses the Montgomery Convention & Visitors Bureau. Sightseeing in Montgomery, via the Lightening Route Trolley, begins here for tours throughout the downtown area.

Muir Stewart
Courtesy of Brown Chambless Architects

Riverfront Development

Spearheaded by the City of Montgomery, the rebirth of Montgomery's Riverfront takes a city of history into a city of the future.

Mary Mclemore

Morning View Plantation

"Morning View," a late nineteenth century Colonial Revival home, was a showplace in the early 1900s with trees from many countries and peacocks on the grounds. The house and lawn gained wide recognition when a picture appeared in a 1931 issue of *National Geographic*. Unfortunately, the house burned in the mid 1960s.

Kathy McLeod

W.A. Gayle Planetarium

W.A. Gayle, mayor of Montgomery in the 1950s, loved nature, animals and Oak Park where the Planetarium, named in his honor, welcomes thousands of visitors annually. His granddaughter painted the picture.

Governor's Mansion
Joseph Stone

Governor's Mansion

Built as a private residence in the early years of the twentieth century, this Neo-Classical mansion became the home for Alabama's governors in the 1950s. Located in the historic Garden District, it reflects the tastes of its period and the talents of architect Weatherly Carter.

Muir Stewart
Courtesy of Barganier Davis Sims Architects

Davis Theatre for the Performing Arts

Originally The Paramount Theatre, it was a "Movie Palace" for the "talkies" or vaudeville shows. It closed in 1976, with the "last picture show" being Gone With The Wind—to reopen again in 1983 as the Davis Theatre for the Performing Arts, under the auspices of Troy State University of Montgomery.

Court Square Fountain

Erected in 1885, this magnificent fountain stands at the historic hub of Montgomery. Court Square was the intersection of the main streets of the two small villages, New Philadelphia and East Alabama, who joined in 1819 to form Montgomery.

Karin Johns

Betty Pinkston

Oakwood Cemetery

The old original Montgomery city cemetery was open to all Montgomery people, and many soldiers and statesmen who shaped area history are buried here — along with some unknowns, hanged felons, and ordinary citizens. It dates back to the early 1800s.

Donnave Lindsey

Girl Overlooking The Marina

Montgomery's Marina on the Alabama River is a favorite scenic spot and a popular recreation area.

Lion's Head

Terra Cotta lion-head masks are mounted on a plinth in the foreground of the Regions Bank building on Commerce Street. The four windows reflect the former Klein and Sons Jeweler.

Carol Barksdale Meredith

Alabama Shakespeare Festival

Located in the English-style Blount Cultural Park, the Alabama Shakespeare Festival is the sixth largest Shakespeare theatre in the world, attracting more than 300,000 visitors annually. It operates year-round, producing many world-class productions, including works of Shakespeare.

Sinclair's and Capri Theatre

Focal point for the Old Cloverdale district, the Capri Theater, called The Clover when built in 1941, was Montgomery's first neighborhood theater and is still vitally active today. Sinclair's, a popular restaurant, was once a Sinclair gas station.

Carol Barksdale Meredith

Historic Commerce Street

From the Alabama River to center city Montgomery, Commerce Street was once the principal wholesale district for Central Alabama. Revitalization began in the 1970s with the restoration of old warehouses.

Joseph Stone

Melissa Tubbs

Oak Park Bridge

The influence of the Olmsted Brothers, sons of landscape architect Frederick Law Olmsted, may have played a role in the development of Oak Park. The foot bridge crossing the pond is similar to elements they sometimes incorporated in their designs.

Steeple, Huntingdon College

Huntingdon College, a co-educational college, celebrated 150 years in 2004 from its early beginnings as Tuskegee Female College. The steeple on Flowers Hall is Tudor Gothic, with gargoyles and weather vanes as ornamentation.

Melissa Tubbs

Joseph Stone

Montgomery Museum of Fine Arts

For over 75 years, the MMFA has been a showcase for the visual arts in Central Alabama. Originally located downtown, it moved to a new home in the Blount Cultural Park in 1988. Today's museum is a successful partnership of public and private commitment to the collecting and preserving of the arts in Montgomery.

F. Scott & Zelda Fitzgerald Museum

Novelist F. Scott Fitzgerald and his wife, Zelda, emblems of the Jazz Age, rented this house in 1931 upon their return from Europe. Although Scott spent much of the time in Hollywood, Zelda worked on her novel, *Save Me the Waltz*, during the year they were here. The house is now a museum, containing memorabilia and programs relating to the famous pair.

Carol Barksdale Meredith

Pike Road Store

Pike Road is one of many small communities surrounding Montgomery that recall a quieter slower place. This store is a prototype of the type of old-time store found in those communities.

Ann Carmichael

F-16 Fighting Falcon

The Alabama Air National Guard, 187th Fighter Wing, received its first F-16 in 1988. The unit has participated in numerous real world contingencies over the last two decades, including Operation Iraqi Freedom. The "Bama Vipers" are recognized worldwide as a premier Air National Guard Fighter Unit.

Bonnie M. Phillips

Entry Gate, Maxwell Air Force Base

Named for Lt. William C. Maxwell of Atmore, Alabama Maxwell Air Force Base is home of the Air University, a professional military education center. Its programs annually affect over half of the United States Air Force.

Connie Watts

Hank Williams Statue

Hank Williams, "Alabama's Troubador," stopped the show at the Grand Ole Opry in Nashville in 1949 with his "Lovesick Blues" and thereafter became a country music legend. He died on New Year's Day 1953, and is buried in Montgomery's Oakwood Annex Cemetery.

Joseph Stone

Bus Hub

The bus hub in downtown Montgomery near Court Square and Colonial Bank is a daily scene of bustling activity.

Bob Adams

Vultee BT – 13/15 "Valiant"

This vintage basic trainer on display at the Gunter Annex to Maxwell Air Force Base represents the planes young pilots nicknamed the "Vibrator" during World War II.

Bonnie M. Phillips

Bonnie M. Phillips

Stone and Wood Bridge

Reminiscent of the English countryside, the wood and stone bridge that crosses a lake in Blount Cultural Park provides a romantic setting, while the Thunderhouse offers shelter and a viewing deck for walkers and runners who frequent the park.

Tim Vaught

Old Alabama Town

This view of the back porches of four "gingerbread cottages" is just a hint of the many excellent and varied nineteenth and early twentieth century architectural gems found in Old Alabama Town, the South's premier history village.

Melissa Tubbs

Bell Building Ornamentation

The Bell Building was constructed in 1906-1910 by Newton J. Bell, Lowndes County planter. He wanted to build a "skyscraper" as a municipal status symbol for Montgomery. This bas relief sculpture on the building reflects the classical style of Amazon-like figures with swords, shields and laurel wreaths.

Carol Barksdale Meredith
Painting: Bibb Graves Bridge/Wetumpka

Autauga, Elmore, Lowndes and Macon Counties

Margrete Barnes Vause

McQueen Smith Farm

McQueen Smith was one of the most successful farmers in Autauga County. This house near Prattville was built in 1895 and has served as family residence and business office for four generations.

Carol Barksdale Meredith

Big Fish House

This house in Elmore County was featured in the 2003 movie *Big Fish*, starring Albert Finney and Jessica Lange. A commercial success, *Big Fish* has increased the probability that more filmmakers will view Alabama locations and stories as subjects for future movies.

Holtville School

Angles, arches, and terra cotta insets in white stucco walls compose the pleasing form of Holtville School in Elmore County. Completed on the eve of the Great Depression, this rural school continues to serve its community with enduring style.

Shirley Esco

Harris-Barrett School

This Macon County two-room country school from 1903-1958 was developed with the help of Booker T. Washington and Tuskegee Institute during a time when 20-80 acre farms were made available to African-American families who wanted to farm and educate their children.

Wendy Slaton

Margrete Barnes Vause

Gurney Mill Tower, Prattville

Paranormal enthusiasts believe that because a little boy once fell down an elevator shaft here and died, his mother still looks for him today. Fire destroyed this historic building in September, 2004.

Carol Barksdale Meredith

Dogtrot Cabin

Dogtrot houses, with rooms separated by open halls, permitted both breezes and dogs to 'trot' through. This handsome example of a once prevalent southern style is in Tallassee, Elmore County.

Bonnie M. Phillips

Capitol Hill Golf Course

This expansive view, with the city of Montgomery in the distance, is seen from Hole #1 on The Judge course at the Capitol Hill Course in Prattville, one of a dazzling collection of golf courses throughout the state called The Robert Trent Jones Golf Trail.

Bob Adams

Downtown Wetumpka

Downtown Wetumpka, with freshly renovated architecture and a home town charm, located on the banks of the Coosa River. Wetumpka derived its name from several Creek Indian words that mean rumbling waters.

Buena Vista

Completed by Captain William Montgomery, the antebellum plantation home, Buena Vista, reflects Federal stylistic influences in its fan lighted entrance doorways and sweeping staircase. Built by Captain William Montgomery, the property has belonged to several others, including the James and Whittaker families and currently (2004) belongs to International Paper Company. The Autauga County Heritage Association maintains it as a historic house museum, making it available for receptions, luncheons and weddings.

Bonnie M. Phillips

The Village Green

The Village Green is the centerpiece of a 15 acre park in the small town of Millbook, a fast-growing community with a country atmosphere in Elmore County.

Shirley Esco

Donnave Lindsey

Betsy Ann Riverboat

Shown here, docked in Wetumpka on the Coosa River, the Betsy Ann Riverboat is an authentic sternwheeler that recalls the romance of a bygone era.

Margrete Barnes Vause

Autauga Creek

Autauga Creek, flowing through Prattville, is namesake for Autauga County—named for the Autauga Indians who once lived along its banks.

Confederate Memorial Oakview Cemetery

The town of Lowndesboro is a treasure-trove of old homes and history, including this 1929 memorial to Confederate soldiers at the entrance to Oakview Cemetery.

Opposite page:
Alabama Confederate Memorial Park

At the northernmost tip of the River Region, in a peaceful setting, is Alabama Confederate Memorial Park. Originally the site of the Alabama Confederate Soldier's Home for Civil War veterans, the park — which includes a museum and nature trail — is now the final resting place for 313 soldiers who had lived there.

Connie Watts

Margrete Barnes Vause

Pratt Manufacturing Gin

Daniel Pratt harnessed the waters of Autauga Creek to power his factory that would become the largest builder of cotton gins in the world. His vision of creating an industrial village in the midst of an agricultural economy took form in 1839 when he laid out the community that would become Prattville.

Connie Watts

C.M.E. Church

The C.M.E. Church in Lowndesboro is topped by Alabama's First Capital Dome and is an example of churches as they were in nineteenth century Alabama.

The Bartram Trail

William Bartram was America's first native born naturalist/artist, whose momentous southern journey (1771-1777) took him through most of the southeastern interior all the way to the Mississippi River. He entered what is now Alabama in 1775 and passed through parts of the River Region.

Connie Watts

Bonnie M. Phillips

Bell-Biggs House

The Bell-Biggs House, a fine example of Queen Anne architecture, is one of many nineteenth century historic homes in Prattville's Daniel Pratt Historic District.

Donnie M. Phillips

Wilderness Park Bamboo Forest

The first park of its type within city limits in the United States, Wilderness Park in Prattville features 2 1/2 acres of giant Oriental bamboo 50-60 feet tall and a wide variety of trees on virgin land preserved intact.

Margrete Barnes Vause

Rawlinson Mill

Located north of Autaugaville on White Water Creek, this old time grist mill (circa 1875) is listed on the National Register of Historic Places. Working grist mills today are as rare as snow in the River Region.

Little Chapel

The antebellum plantation chapel in Prattville has theme gardens developed and maintained by the Autauga County Master Gardeners Association for the enjoyment of the entire community.

Bonnie M. Phillips

Cam Walker

Lowndes County Courthouse

The Lowndes County Courthouse, finished in 1858 is the focal point of the quiet, charming town of Hayneville—the county seat of Lowndes County. Built in the Greek Revival style, the structure reflects the tremendous plantation-based wealth of antebellum Lowndes County.

Fort Toulouse/Jackson

This cannon is one of many artifacts on view at the Fort Toulouse-Jackson Military Park. Comprised of the French Fort Toulouse (1717-1763) and Fort Jackson, and constructed by Andrew Jackson at the conclusion of the Creek-American War of 1813-1814, the historic site hosts a variety of interpretive events.

Bonnie M. Phillips

Carol Barksdale Meredith

Mt. Vernon Mills

Although Tallassee's Mt. Vernon Mills now occupy these modern buildings, their history goes back to the antebellum Tallassee Mills. Dating from 1844, the original operation produced textiles and during the Civil War Confederate uniforms and the famous Tallassee Carbines. These mills are the longest continous manufacturers of yarns in the United States today.

Bob Adams
Painting: "The 301 Club"/Dexter Avenue United Methodist Church

Life in the River Region

Paulette Riley

Curb Market Couple

Archie and Emma Dennis, for well over 50 years, have been vendors at the Montgomery Curb Market; Archie often entertained customers with tales of long ago. Emma cans peach pickles, preserves, and delicious soup mix.

Paulette Riley

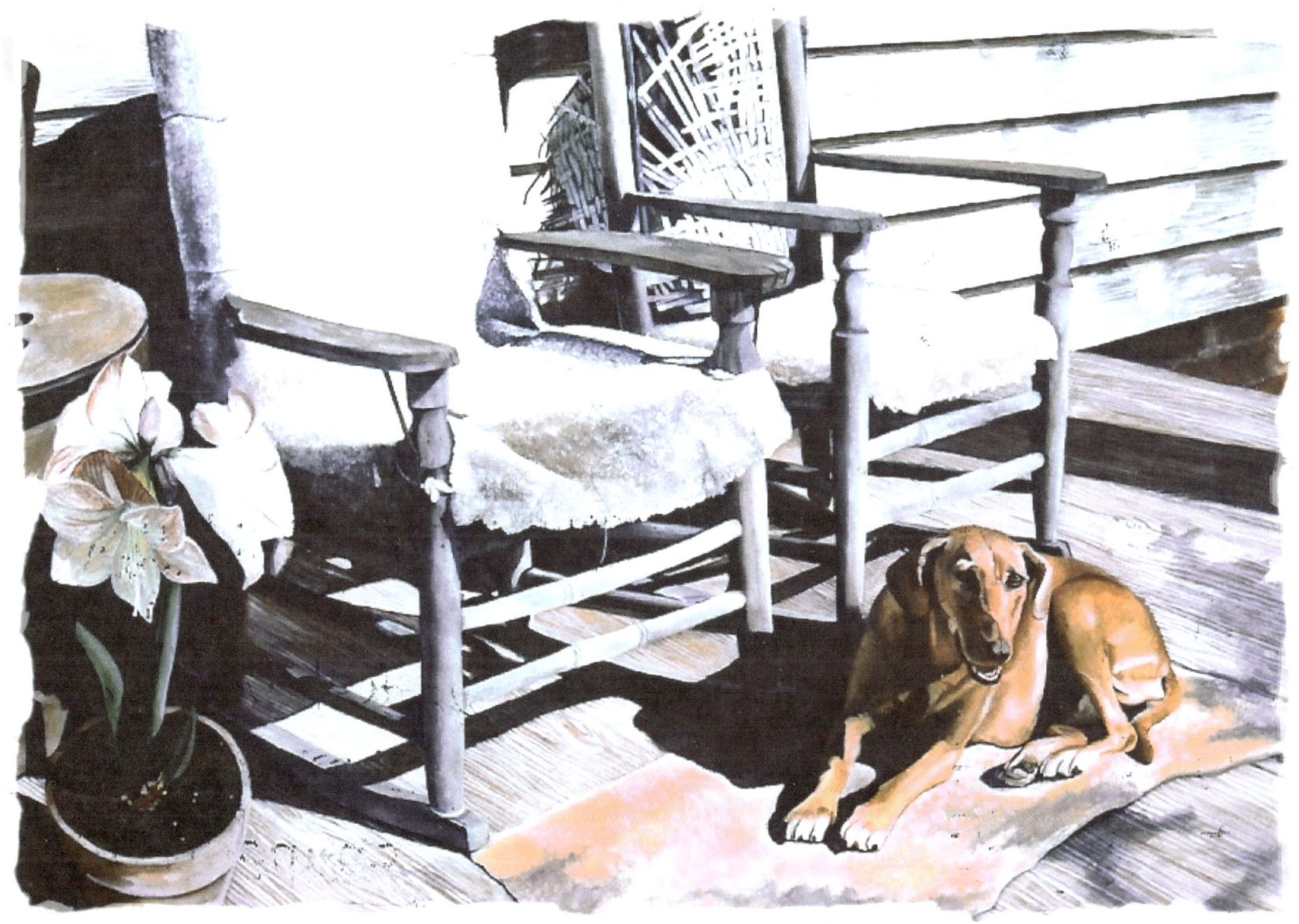

Paulette Riley

Dog and Rocking Chairs

Rocking chairs and sleepy dogs are often "Soul Mates" on front porches that are also adorned by colorful flowers in planters, pots, or even cans.

Night Baseball

Montgomery's revitalized Riverfront includes a new minor league baseball stadium, where the game can be enjoyed under the "stars falling on Alabama."

Bob Adams

Connie Watts

Chalk Art

Children make chalk drawings on the parking places at the Montgomery Museum of Fine Arts during the annual Flimp Festival, the "Museum's Gift to the Community" the first Saturday in May.

Bob Adams

Jubilee CityFest

Jubilee CityFest, an annual 3-day weekend close to Memorial Day, features fireworks and an outdoor concert by the Montgomery Symphony, arts and crafts exhibits, headline entertainment, a PraiseFest for the faith community, and the 8K / 2 mile Run Walk through the streets of Montgomery. Can you find the Tortoise and the Hare in the painting?

Walking in the Park

As a father and son walk in Blount Cultural Park, it almost seems the young boy would prefer to join the fun exhibited in the "Puddle Jumpers" outdoor sculpture by Glenna Goodacre.

Connie Watts

First Baptist Church

Modeled after a cathedral in Florence, Italy, First Baptist has played an influential role in the historic, cultural, and religious life of Montgomery and the South.

Jospeh Stone

Fishing

Fishing is a popular pastime in the River Region, whether spending a Sunday afternoon at a pond like the one in Lagoon Park or out on a lake searching for that big bass.

Paulette Riley

Soul of Henry

Music can be enjoyed by everyone in the community because of the contribution and dedication of many. The sounds of all genre can be heard year-round through educational programs, in churches, and public performances.

Paulette Riley

Pisgah Primitive Baptist Church

Constituted in 1842 in a log building with 6 charter members, the present Colonial Revival building in south Montgomery County was completed in 1931.

Neal Brantley

"Good Morning Miss Willis"

A tradition at Wetumpka Elementary School, students pass by the principal each day for a mutual "Good Morning."

Bob Adams

Adams Hudson

First United Methodist Church, Cloverdale

The congregation of this beautiful church on a tree-filled campus in Old Cloverdale celebrated 175 years of service in 2004.

Richard Millman

"Firebird" Ballerina

The Montgomery Ballet performs "The Firebird" at Performance On The Green in July, in addition to "The Nutcracker Suite" in December and other performances throughout the year.

Karin Johns

Alabama Dance Theatre

Alabama Dance Theatre, located at the Armory Learning Arts Center, trains students in the disciplined art of dance and produces professional performances at the Davis Theatre for the Performing Arts.

Karen Seamon

Karin Johns

Lagoon Park Golf Course

The Lagoon Park Golf Course, designed for the City of Montgomery, has been rated one of the nation's Best Public Courses by Golf Digest.

Bob Adams

Jane Jacobs

Alabama National Fair Panorama / Racing Pigs

Alabama's National Fair in Montgomery—with its food, amusement rides, livestock competitions, and stage entertainment—is a major event each October.

Police on Bicycles / Parking Meter & Meter Maid

You don't have to look far for a law enforcement presence in downtown Montgomery.

Bob Adams

Bob Adams

Old Farmer

Farming has always been important in the River Region; as an elderly man reminisces about the good life on the farm.

Paulette Riley

Trinity Presbyterian Church

Organized as a congregation in 1891, the current church at Felder Avenue and Hull Street was modeled after the First Presbyterian Church of Philadelphia and dedicated in 1952.

Richard Millman

St. John's Episcopal Church

Listed on the National Register of Historic Places, St. John's is the oldest Episcopal church in Montgomery. The congregation dates from 1834 and the building from 1835.

Bob Adams

Macedonia Baptist Church

The biblical message "the fields are white for harvest" seems to ring true in this view of the Macedonia Baptist Church near Prattville, surrounded by cotton fields in full bloom.

St. Peter's Catholic Church

The largest Roman Catholic Church in the area, St. Peter's celebrated its 150th anniversary in 2004.

Joseph Stone

Fort Deposit United Methodist Church

Fort Deposit United Methodist Church in southern Lowndes County, beautifully distinctive with its double front staircases, is a focal point for historic Fort Deposit — established as a supply fort in 1813 by General Claiborne, under orders from Andrew Jackson.

Tim Vaught

Church of the Ascension

On Easter Sunday 1910, the congregation of the Episcopal Church of the Ascension first worshipped in their new edifice. Designed by Ralph Adam Cram, a leading exponent of Gothic Revival architecture, the church is on McDonough Street in the historic Garden District.

Bonnie M. Phillips

Bob Adams

Montgomery Curb Market

A popular place for locals and visitors to the area, the Montgomery Curb Market is open year round with vendors selling fresh vegetables, baked goods, and flowers.

Jane Jacobs

Shirley Esco

Cain's Chapel United Metohdist Church

Cain's Chapel in Deatsville, Elmore County is the oldest continuous church congregation in the River Region, dating back to 1817. Originally a log structure built by Elisha Milton Cain for his family to worship, today's church is the fourth and is attended by members from several counties throughout the area

The Artists

Bob Adams
334-365-1647
918 Skidmore Ave.
Prattville, AL 36066
Pages 35,53,64,79,82,83,86
90,91,95,98,108

David Keith Braly
334-264-8906
2052 Ridge Ave.
Montgomery, AL 36106
www.davidbraly.com
Pages 25,103

Neal Brantley
334-262-7004
1215 S. McDonough St.
Montgomery, AL 36104
nealbrantley@aol.com
Page 86

Ann C. Carmichael
334-272-8752
3321 Royal Carniage Dr.
Montgomery, AL 36066
anncarmi@bellsouth.net
Page 50

Catherine Cope
334-279-8869
212 Milly Branch Court
Pike Road, AL 36064
copeworks@hudsonink.com
Page 24

Shirley Esco
334-569-3909
400 Culpepper Rd.
Deatsville, AL 36022
dsesco9696@aol.com
Pages 60,65,100,107

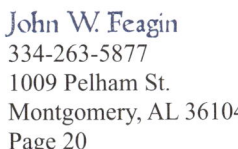
John W. Feagin
334-263-5877
1009 Pelham St.
Montgomery, AL 36104
Page 20

Jane L. Jacobs
334-281-1756
1352 Devonshire Dr.
Montgomery, AL 36116
janellow@juno.com
Pages 90,99

Karin E. Johns
334-279-6876
3928 Oak Ave.
Montgomery, AL 36109
charlesaj@earthlink.net
Pages 37,42,88,89

Adams Hudson
334-262-1110
805 Felder Ave.
Montgomery, AL 36106
adams@hudsonink.com
Pages 4,87

Donnave Lindsey
334-288-1632
3774 Audobon Rd.
Montgomery, AL 36111
donnavelindsey@yahoo.com
Pages 43,66

Mary Campbell McLemore
334-265-5070
2330 Rosemont Place
Montgomery, AL 36066
Page 39

Kathie McLeod
334-264-6838
2504 Agnew St.
Montgomery, AL 36106
kmcleod49@yahoo.com
Page 40

Carol Barksdale Meredith
334-567-7056
245 Jackson Trace Rd.
Titus, AL 36080
bdaleart@aol.com
Pages 16,18,22,45,46,50,57
59,62,78

Richard Millman
334-887-6428
736 Brenda Ave.
Auburn, AL 36830
millmmm@charter.net
Pages 9,10,11,12,17,21,87
94,106,108,109,111

Bonnie Phillips
256-207-2432
1700 Fulton Gap Rd.
Sylacauga, AL 35150
phillipshonnie@bellsouth.net
Pages 51,53,54,63,65,73,74,76
77,97,105

Betty Pinkston
334-279-6181
6416 Ashton Circle
Montgomery, AL 36117
bpink01@knology.com
Page 43

Paulette M. Riley
334-333-1080
110 Kensington Ct.
Dothan, AL 36303
prileyart@centurytel.net
Pages 33,36,80,81,85,92,
104,110,Back Cover

Karen Seamon
334-361-9965
1845 Co. Rd. 107
Prattville, AL 36066
karenseamon@charter.net
Page 88

Wendy A. Slaton
334-315-3092
P.O. Box 827
Hayesville, NC. 28904
joeslaton@aol.com
Page 60

Joseph Stone
334-265-8808
2039 Hazel Hedge Ln.
Montgomery, AL 36106
josephstone@bellsouth.net
Pages 13,15,19,41,46,49,52
84,96,113

Melissa B. Tubbs
334-538-7800
327 Rose Ln.
Montgomery, AL 36104-5638
inkartist2@charter.net
Pages 29,44,47,48,56,93

Mary Walton Upchurch
334-834-3409
marywalton@mindspring.com
Page 36

Tim Vaught
334-262-9316
reddog39@hiwaay.net
Pages 55, 97

Margrete Barnes Vause
850-785-3354
100 Hamilton Ave.
Panama City, FL 32401
Pages 58,61,67,70,75

Cam Walker
334-872-2795
473 County Rd. 820
Selma, AL 36701
artcam@bellsouth.net
Page 77

Connie Watts
428 Forest Hills Dr.
Childersburg, AL 35044
Pages 51,68,69,71,72,83,
84,104,109

Index

A
Alabama Confederate Memorial Park 69
Alabama Dance Theatre 88
Alabama National Fair 90
Alabama River 7
Alabama Shakespeare Festival 45
Alabama State Capitol 35
Alabama Supreme Court 34
Approaching Montgomery 36
Autauga Creek 67

B
Bell-Biggs House 73
Bell Building 56
Betsy Ann Riverboat 66
Bibb Graves Bridge/Wetumpka 57
Big Fish House 59
Blount Cultural Park 84
Buena Vista 65
Bus Hub 53

C
C.M.E. Church 71
Cain's Chapel United Methodist Church
    Church 100
Capitol Hill Golf Course 63
Carnegie Library 25
Chalk Art 83
Church of Ascension 97
Confederate Memorial, Oakview
    Cemetery 68
Coosa Street Warehouse 24
Court Square Fountain 42
Court Square to the Capitol 33
Creek Indian Village of Takubatchie 16
Curb Market Couple 80

D
Dexter Avenue Baptist Church 20
Dogtrot Cabin 62
Dog and Rocking Chairs 81
Downtown Wetumpka 64
Dr. Martin Luther King Jr. house 31

E
Early Morning on the Alabama River 36
Entry Gates, Maxwell Air Force Base 51

F
"Firebird Ballerina" 88
F-16 Fighting Falcon 51
F. Scott & Zelda Fitzgerald Museum 50
Figh-Picket-Barnes School House 12
First Baptist Church 84
First United Methodist Church, Cloverdale 87
Fort Deposit United Methodist Church 97
Fort Toulouse/Jackson 77

G
"Good Morning Miss Willis" 86
Girl Overlooking The Marina 43
Governor's Mansion 41
Gurney Mill Tower, Prattville 61

H
Hank Williams Statue 52
Harris-Barrett School 60
Historic Commerce Street 46
Holtville School 63

J
Jubiliee CityFest 83

L
Lagoon Park 85
Lagoon Park Golf Course 89
Lightning Route Trolleys 19
Little Chapel 76
Lowndes County Courthouse 77

M
Macedonia Baptist Church 95
McQueen Smith Farm 58
Meter Maid 91
Montgomery Curb Market 99
Montgomery Museum of Fine Arts 49
Morning View Plantation 39
Mt. Vernon Mills 78

N
Night Baseball 82

O
Oakwood Cemetery 43
Oak Park Bridge 47
Oak Park Pavilion 9
Old Alabama Town 55
Old Farmer 92
Old Montgomery Courthouse 11
Ordeman Townhouse 15

P
Pike Road Store 50
Pisgah Primitive Baptist Church 86
Police on Bicycles 91
Pratt Manufacturing Gin 70

R
Rawlinson Mill 75
Regions Bank 44
Riverfront Development 38
Rosa Parks 32

S
Shotgun House 22
Sinclair's and Capri Theatre 46
Soul of Henry 85
St. John's Episcopal Church 94
St. Peter's Catholic Church 96
Steamboat Alabama 10
Steeple, Huntingdon College 48
Stone and Wood Bridge, Blount Cultural
    Park 54

T
"The 301 Club"/Dexter Avenue United
    Methodist Church 79
The Bartram Trail 72
The Civil Rights Memorial 29
The Teague House 21
The Tuskegee Airmen 26
The Village Green 65
Thomas W. Oliver Gin 18
Trinity Presbyterian Church 93

U
Union Station 37

V
Vultee BT-13/15 "Valiant" 53

W
W.A. Gayle Planetarium 40
Walking for Freedom 28
Wilderness Park Bamboo Forest 74
Wright Brother 13

Artists not pictured.

Sheridan Glenn
Contact info not available.
Page 35

Rev. Tony Scott
334-324-6484
Pages 26, 28

Ruth Soller
303-469-2072
solleroriginals@juno.net
Page 32

Yvonne Williams
800-718-7508
yvonne@innerstream.net
Page 31

David Braly

Montgomery County, organized in 1816, bears the name of Major Lemuel P. Montgomery and was much larger originally, but donated much of it's land for the creation of other river region counties. One of the earliest of these was Autuaga County that came into existence in 1818 bearing the name of a creek and the name of the Indian village of Atagi. Lowndes County, named for William Lowndes, South Carolina statesman, and created from parts of Montgomery, Dallas and Butler counties, dates from 1830. The Alabama Legislature created Macon County, honoring Revolutionary hero Nathaniel Macon, Creek land session; Elmore County, named for early settler John Archer Elmore, has existed since 1866.

Like Montgomery's early founders, her contemporary leaders are ardent about the place in which they reside. These community leaders share enthusiasm and dedication to a community whose variety of histories, traditions, and wealth of cultural diversity provides something special for everyone. Whether seeking an art gallery or museum or simply sitting down to a comforting down-home southern meal, you'll fit right in. Welcome, come on in!

Indigo Custom Publishing gratefully acknowledges the companies, institutions, and organizations represented here that have willingly and graciously given their steadfast and earnest support to the fruition of the *Montgomery & The River Region Sketchbook* project.

Alfa Insurance

Connie Watts

"Becoming a part of the Alfa Insurance family is about effecting change in people's lives—whether it is that of a customer, and employee, or a member of the local community. For the Alfa family, however, being part of the communnity means more that providing insurance coverage. It also means supporting the communities in which Alfa customers work and live."

—Jerry Newby
President/CEO

Auburn University Montgomery

Paulette Riley

"The legacy of shaping lives is one shared by the faculty and staff at AUM. I feel a responsibility to our students to help them succeed in a competitve world."

—Dr. Anne Permaloff
Political Science Professor

Barganier Davis Sims Architects Associated

Bonnie Phillips

"The culture of BDS promotes civic and charitable activites, such as Leadership Montgomery, a nonprofit, nonpartisan 501(c)(3) educational organization, which provides unique opportunities to people who are at different stages of their lives to become well-informed community leaders. All of the partners believe in service to their community not only through the firm, but also through civic clubs and churches."

—Jim Barganier
Principal Architect

Blue Cross/Blue Shield of Alabama

Richard Millman

"Blue Cross and Blue Shield of Alabama is committed to health, safety, education and wellness, and continues to make a strong impact in the communities it serves. The company provides numerous health management programs, public information campaigns, grants for reading and education initiatives, and thousands of hours of in-kind employee volunteer services for tutoring and mentoring in local school systems."

—Phillip Popee
President/CEO

Cain's Chapel United Methodist Church

Shirley Esco

"Our greatest strength is ministering to children and youth—the future of the church. We are blessed to have creative leadership, an exceptional choir, and Bible programs."

—Marie "Bitsy" Nelson

Colonial Bank

Barclay Burns

"We plan to continue to offer the best of both worlds to the banking customer: the deep resources of a strong regional bank without the cumbersome bureaucracy of a mammoth bank, while offering the personal touch that customers normally expect from a community bank."

—Robert E. Lowder
Chairman/CEO

Dexter Avenue United Methodist Church

Bob Adams

"We believe that the Christian faith makes a positive difference in peoples' lives. Our ministry programs and services are designed to bring inner peace in a chaotic and uncertain world. We seek to live out our worship and faith full of love and joy."

—Dennis Carlson
Pastor

First United Methodist Church

Richard Millman

"Those who have claimed First United Methodist Church as their home of Christian fellowship have discovered a powerful way not only to become an active part of the city of Montgomery, but also to reach far beyond the city limits. The only reason a person attending First United Methodist Church would ever want to leave would be to tell others about the wonderful fellowship and powerful ministry going on within this church family."

—Dr. Karl K. Stegall
Senior Pastor

Lowder New Homes

Richard Millman

"From the start, Lowder New Homes has shown that we care about the Montgomery area," Jimmy Lowder concluded. "We've demonstrated leadership in the new home market and in community service and have seen our efforts make a difference. We're proud of that and proud to be part of a region that offers a wonderful quality of life and great opportunity to everyone."

—*Jimmy Lowder*
Chairman

McPhillips, Shinbaum & Gill LLP

Connie Watts

"We are The People's Law Firm," says founder Julian McPhillips. "We don't represent any big corporations or insurance companies; we don't represent any agencies or departments of state and we don't represent the city or county of Montgomery. We just represent the people who have problems with them all."

—*Julian McPhillips*

Prudential Ballard Realty

Barclay Burns

"We are sensitive to our clients' and customers' needs. We listen to them. An impressive number of our projects have been completed at or under budget. Our many years of experience and an enthusiastic, professional staff help our clients' and customers' dreams become reality."

—Jimmie Ann Campbell
President

Regions Bank

Barclay Burns

"It may sound old-fashioned, but we base our relations with our customers on traditional Southern hospitality. Our focus is on the customer, and on doing whatever we can to tailor our services to meet their needs. We take pride in the fact that our efforts make a real contribution to the lives of Montgomery residents and we strive every day to be Montgomery's hometown bank."

—Mildred V. Houston
Sr. Vice President

Sterne, Agee & Leach, Inc.

Paulette Riley

"Sterne, Agee & Leach takes pride in the fact that it is the oldest and largest native Alabama investment firm. Building wealth for its clients is the objective of Sterne, Agee & Leach and dedication to that purpose continues today."

—*Chappell H.L. Hill*
Managing Director

Summit America

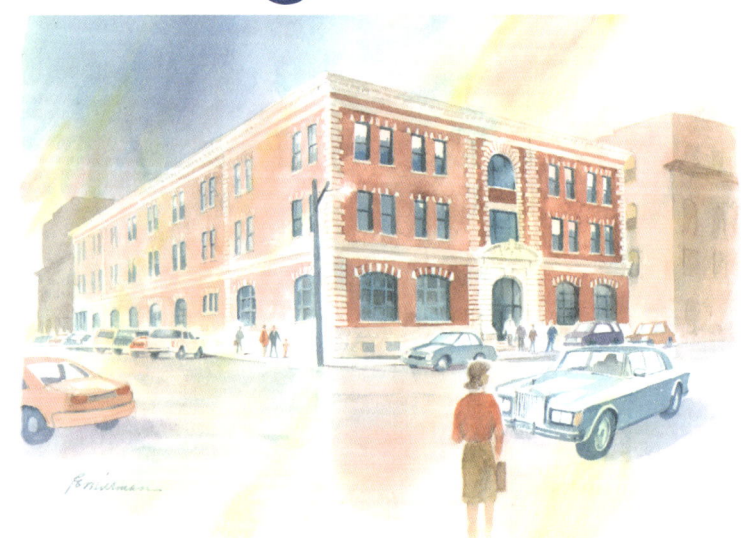

Richard Millman

"It's not about any one person, but rather a combined effort of a talented team. That is a core value that I think is very important in an organization and it's really why we've been able to accomplish so much in a fairly short period of time."

—*Daniel Hughes*
CEO

Trinity Presbyterian Church

Richard Millman

"Trinity Presbyterian Church's three-pronged, heartfelt mission is to glorify God through simple, God-centered worship, to equip church members through faithful teaching, and to aggressively eveanglize both at home and abroad. Put more succinctly, the church aims to exalt the Savior, expound the Scriptures, and exhort the sinner."

—*Laura Steiner*

WCOV FOX 20

Barclay Burns

"Supporting the communities in which we live and work creates a great deal of goodwill. In turn, people feel more comfortable supporting us because we're supporting them," said Woods. The station donates tens of thousands of dollars each year to various non-profits groups to promote their message or cause, including the Salvation Army, the Montgomery Zoo, the Red Cross, Boy Scouts, United Way, and the Armed Forces, as well as numerous local organizations. An achievement of which both Woods and the station are particulary proud of is Woods' recent involvement in the massive implementation of the Amber Alert system for the state of Alabama."

—*David Woods*
President

WSFA-12

Joseph Stone

"Coverage, Community, Commitment" is the slogan that has guided WSFA 12 in Montgomery for fifty years.

Since WSFA 12 signed on the air on Christmas Day in 1954, the station has had a serious commitment to news coverage. Local news continues to be the cornerstone of this NBC affiliate, and many of the nearly 100 employees are dedicated to delivering top quality coverage to viewers, with a focus on advocacy journalism. In the beginning, WSFA 12 aired a daily one half-hour newscast. Today, WSFA 12 airs more than twenty-one hours of local newscasts each week.

Reinvesting in the community has always been a priority for WSFA 12. The American Red Cross, the American Cancer Society's Relay for Life, the Alabama Shakespeare Festival Theater and "12s Day of Giving" annual holiday fundraiser are just a few of the many organizations and events the station consistently sponsors.

Vice President and General Manager Hoyt Andres is proud of the station's involvement in the community, and of the fact that WSFA 12 has consistently been ranked by Nielsen as one of the top television stations in America. Mr. Andres said, "We listen to our viewers, and I believe that supports our goal to be the dominant local news and information provider in southeastern Alabama. Our website is a very integral part of our business. We're always seeking to be better, and do better for our viewers and website users, and provide them with information that's relevant to their lives."

WSFA 12, 12 East Delano Avenue, Montgomery, Alabama, 334-288-1212, www.wsfa.com

Alagasco

Joseph Stone

Alabama Gas Corporation (Alagasco) got its start in Montgomery over 150 years ago. From lighting the streets with manufactured gas to serving homes and businesses with natural gas, the company has become the largest natural gas utility in Alabama.

Alagasco has experienced many changes since 1852. Today it is a subsidiary of Birmingham's Energen Corporation. The company serves over 463,000 customers in the state, including approximately 87,000 in Autauga, Elmore and Montgomery counties.

Alagasco is committed to providing excellent customer service. "It is important to us to provide a working environment that encourages innovation and supports our employees' abilities to provide superior customer service. We also strive to be a responsible corporate citizen by taking an active role in the communities we serve," said Steve Chapman, vice president – Montgomery operations.

Employees are involved with different organizations in the Montgomery area including: Habitat for Humanity, American Cancer Society, March of Dimes, Salvation Army, Joy to Life Foundation, American Red Cross, Adopt-A-School, American Heart Association and United Way. Alagasco is also a co-sponsor of Project SHARE (Service to Help Alabamians with Relief on Energy). The program raises money to help thousands of Alabamians pay their energy bills.

Alagasco has maintained a reliable energy source for Alabama and thanks to the loyal and satisfied customers they will provide the same for many more years to come.